D1632312

If the sea was in the sky . . .

Poetry collection 5

Imagine

ANONYMOUS

If the sea was in the sky,
And trees grew underground,
And if all fish had giant teeth,
And all the cows were round;
If birds flew backwards all the time,
And vultures ruled the land.
If bricks poured down instead of rain,
If all there was was sand;
If every man had seven heads
And we spoke Double Dutch,
And if the sun came out at night,
I wouldn't like it much.

Published by Evans Brothers Limited
2A Portman Mansions
Chiltern Street
London
W1U 6NR

© Evans Brothers Limited 2002

Printed in Hong Kong by Wing King Tong Co. Ltd.

Editor: Su Swallow
Design: Neil Sayer
Production: Jenny Mulvanny

British Library Cataloguing in Publication Data
If the Sea was in the Sky ...
Poetry collection 5
1. Children's poetry, English
I. Waters, Fiona
821.9'14'08

ISBN 0 237 52126 1

Dedication

For John Hubbard,
best of dinosaurs,
with much love.

If the sea was in the sky . . .

Poetry collection 5

compiled by
Fiona Waters

illustrated by
Tracy Fennell

EVANS BROTHERS LIMITED

Contents

INSTRUCTIONS FOR GROWING POETRY (FOUND ON THE BACK OF THE PACKET)

Tony Mitton

Shut your eyes.
Open your mind
Look inside.
What do you find?
Something funny?
Something sad?
Something beautiful,
mysterious, mad?
Open your ears.
Listen well.
A word or phrase
begins to swell?
Catch its rhythm.
Hold its sound.
Gently, slowly
roll it round.
Does it please you?
Does it tease you?
Does it ask
to grow and spread?
Now those little
words are sprouting
poetry
inside your head.

POETRY
JANET S WONG

'What you study in school?' my grandfather asks.

'Poetry,' I say, climbing high to pick a large ripe
lemon off the top limb.

'Po-tree,' he says. 'It got fruit?'

BIRDFOOT'S GRAMP
JOSEPH BRUCHAC

The old man
must have stopped our car
two dozen times to climb out
and gather into his hands
the small toads blinded
by our light and leaping,
live drops of rain.

      The rain was falling,
      a mist about his white hair
      and I kept saying
      you can't save them all,
      accept it, get back in
      we've got places to go.

But, leathery hands full
of wet brown life,
knee deep in the summer
roadside grass,
he just smiled and said
they have places to go, too.

11

GRANDAD'S CLOTHES

JOHN FOSTER

'What did you wear
when you were my age, Grandpa?'
I asked.
'Did you wear T-shirts?
Did you wear jeans and trainers?'

Grandpa smiled
and got out his photo album.
He showed me a picture
of a small boy
in a white cotton shirt,
short trousers and long socks.

'That's what I wore
all the year round,'
he said.
'Only grown-ups wore long trousers.'

'Didn't your knees get cold?'
I asked.

'Of course, they did,'
he said.
'We just had to put up with it.
Nowadays, grown-ups have got more sense.'

EARWINGS

BRIAN PATTEN

When I was little
My mother wore earwings.
Each night
She would creep to my bedroom window,
Open it,
And taking me gently in her arms
Glide off into the night.

WHAT IS UNDER?

TONY MITTON

What is under the grass, Mummy,
what is under the grass?
Roots and stones and rich soil
where the loamy worms pass.

What is over the sky, Mummy,
what is over the sky?
Stars and planets and boundless space,
but never a reason why.

What is under the sea, Mummy,
what is under the sea?
Weird and wet and wondrous things,
too deep for you and me.

What is under my skin, Mummy,
what is under my skin?
Flesh and blood and a frame of bones
and your own dear self within.

OH DEAR, MUM!
BARRY BUCKINGHAM

Mum telephoned the zoo,
and then the RSPCA,
and when they came
they couldn't help but laugh.
For Dad had shouted:
    'Shut the door!
      There's such a terrible draught!'
Mum thought he'd said:
    'A terrible giraffe.'

MY MONSTROUS BEAR
GERVASE PHINN

When I was small,
My father would pretend to be a monstrous bear.
He'd crawl about the floor on all fours
And his great ferocious eyes
Would stare and glare, searching for me.
He'd roar and roar
And growl and grunt,
And I would hide behind the chair,
And squeal and squirm
And feel the hair on my head stand up,
Excited in my fear.
He'd pretend not to see me
And lumber off and curl up on the rug
And snore and snore.
I would creep so quietly
And snuggle up, deep between his great warm paws.
My monstrous bear would hold me tightly
Keeping me from harm.

14

THE MARTIANS HAVE TAKEN MY BROTHER

Rowena Sommerville

The Martians have taken my brother,
I must say I'm glad that they did,
I know it seems hard on my mother,
but he was such a pain of a kid.

He kept pinching things from the larder,
he kept making smells in the loo,
and though I tried harder and harder,
I just couldn't like him - could you?

The Martians have got him well hidden
(he's locked in the shed for the day),
And Dad says the shed is forbidden,
so I've thrown the shed key away.

I know that he'll bang on the window,
I know that he'll yell and he'll shout,
I think that he'll have to stay in though,
'cos the Martians just won't let him out!

Oh dear! Mum's back from the shop now,
I've seen her walk in through the gate,
I suppose all the fun has to stop now,
Oh no! - she's come in - it's too late!

I wish I could rescue my brother,
I wish I could unlock the shed,
'cos if I get caught by my mother,
She might put me in there instead!

15

THE BABYSITTER

LINDSAY MacRAE

It was clear
From the moment
They walked out the door
That Tracey
Had never done
This job before.

Until they came home
She patiently sat
On me
       my little brother
              and the cat.

THE WICKED STEPMOTHER

LINDSAY MacRAE

I expected her to wear hobnail boots
Beneath a stiff brown skirt.
I expected her to screech
Like a throttled parrot:
'No you can't go to the ball
              the ball'

Or:
'Scrub that floor again!'

I just knew she would offer me
Shiny, poisoned apples;
Hide all my party invitations;
Spend hours asking the mirror
Leading questions

Then take me into a forest
And leave me there.

I pictured her waiting
For the postman
To deliver a parcel
Containing my torn-out heart.

I thought I would have to
Grow my hair
Until it was long enough
To hang out of high windows.

I imagined pinning all my hopes
On a mountaineering prince
Armed with a chainsaw
And a first aid manual.
Or the kindness of seven
short men.

So imagine my surprise
When an ordinary-looking person arrived
Who likes fairy tales too.

17

MUM

Andrew Fusek Peters & Polly Peters

She's a:

Sadness stealer
Cut-knee healer
Hug-me-tighter
Wrongness righter
Gold-star carer
Chocolate sharer
    (well, sometimes!)

Hamster feeder
Bedtime reader
Great game player
Night-fear slayer
Treat dispenser
Naughty sensor
    (how come she always knows?)

She's my
Never-glum
Constant-chum
Second-to-none
(We're under her thumb!)
Mum!

DAD

Andrew Fusek Peters & Polly Peters

He's a:

Tall-story weaver
Full-of-fib fever
Bad-joke teller
Ten-decibel yeller
Baggy-clothes wearer
Pocket-money bearer
Nightmare banisher
Hurt-heart vanisher

Bear hugger
Biscuit mugger
Worry squasher
Noisy nosher
Lawn mower
Smile sower

Football mad
Fashion sad
Not half bad
So glad I had
My dad!

GRANDPA

BERLIE DOHERTY

Grandpa's hands are as rough as garden sacks
And as warm as pockets.
His skin is crushed paper round his eyes
Wrapping up their secrets.

POTTING SHED

JEANNE WILLIS

Packets of seeds,
Buckets of weeds,
Onions on a string,
Bulbs in bowls,
A cure for moles,
A book on gardening.
Lots of pots,
Forget-Me-Nots,
Seedlings in a tray,
Trowels and spades,
Lawnmower blades,
And cans of greenfly spray.
Roots and shoots,
And muddy boots,
Tomatoes turning red,
My favourite smell in all the world
Is Grandad's potting shed.

I PLANTED SOME SEEDS

Colin McNaughton

I planted some seeds
in my garden today.
They haven't come up yet,
I hope they're okay.

Should I dig them all up,
Take them back to the shop?
Ask for my money back,
Say they're a flop?

Perhaps they were faulty,
Perhaps they were duff,
Maybe they haven't
Been watered enough.

I planted some seeds
In my garden today.
They haven't come up yet,
I hope they're okay.

UNICORN

James Kirkup

I met a unicorn today –
four silver hooves all gleaming bright.

His coat was of a pearly grey,
his mane and tail of purest white.

His eyes were dark and warm and round
with eyelashes of fine pale silk.
He gently pawed the frosty ground
and snorted plumes like spectral milk.

And from the centre of his brow
one twisted horn of purest glass
sparked beneath a snowy bough.
– I watched him slowly turn, and pass

into the sombre forest glade,
where he looked back at me, as though
to tell me not to be afraid,
and trust the crystal horn's soft glow.

I followed him, and very soon
he paused, till I reached his side.
Then, with the rising of the moon,
we set off on a wild night ride.

All night I lay along his back,
grasping that horn of purest glass.
We galloped down each forest track
till dawn sparked diamonds from the grass.

Then O! the frost all melted, and the snow:
the leaves all flashed with crystal dew!
But he had vanished – where I do not know …
Could this have been a dream? Or was it true?

GREEN MAN IN THE GARDEN

CHARLES CAUSLEY

Green man in the garden
 Staring from the tree,
Why do you look so long and hard
 Through the pane at me?

Your eyes are dark as holly,
 Of sycamore your horns,
Your bones are made of elder-branch,
 Your teeth are made of thorns.

Your hat is made of ivy-leaf,
 Of bark your dancing shoes,
And evergreen and green and green
 Your jacket and shirt and trews.

Leave your house and leave your land,
 And throw away the key,
And never look behind, he creaked,
 And come and live with me.

I bolted up the window,
 I bolted up the door,
I drew the blind that I should find
 The green man never more.

But when I softly turned the stair
 As I went up to bed,
I saw the green man standing there.
 Sleep well, my friend, he said.

24

THE DRAGON ON THE WALL

Stanley Cook

A bright green dragon comes in at the door
And crawls along the classroom wall.
He must be lost
Or need a rest
For he never came into the classroom before.

His body is hard as a fist with nobbly scales.
He could pull down a tree that he hooked with his tail.
He rests on the wall, his mouth open wide,
Puffing and panting flames from inside.

His green silky wings are raised on his back,
Ready to come down in one big flap
To carry him out of the open window
When no one's there to see him go.

When we leave him on his own
Does he fly home
In a streak of light
Through the black of the night
To see that his cave is safe
With all its bright shining gold?

DRAGONFLIES

JOAN POULSON

They used to fly
over all the ponds
in summer, granny says –

like sparkling sapphire helicopters,
purple aeroplanes,
with eyes of bright topaz,
wings flashing emerald light,
brightening the countryside
in their jewelled flight.

Sun-glow brilliance winging
over every pond,
someday I hope to see one
– smallest last dragon.

THE GREAT WHITE HORSE

JEAN KENWARD

Does the great horse shine,
the horse on the hill
with his white chalk coat?
Does he shine there still?

Does he rise at night
from the grey-green grass
and gallop a bit?
Do you see him pass?

Do you hear his hooves
go thudding by
when the moon looks down
from a blue-black sky?

Does he kick the stars up,
sparking bright?
Or sleep . . . alone . . .
in the blue-black night?

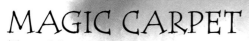

MAGIC CARPET
TONY MITTON

Magic carpet,
your bright colours
delight the eye.

Your moons and stars
and midnight blues
sing of the sky.

Magic carpet,
kept in the cupboard,
I hear you sigh.

Let me unroll
your magic pattern
and help you fly.

28

HARRY HOBGOBLIN'S SUPERSTORE

DAVID HARMER

You want a Gryphon's feather
Or a spell to change the weather?
A pixilating potion
That helps you fly an ocean?
Some special brew of magic
To supercharge your broomstick?
Witches wizards, why not pop
Into Harry's one-stop shop?

Tins of powdered dragons' teeth
Bottled beetles, newts.
Freeze-dried cobwebs, cats and rats
Screaming mandrake roots.
Lizard skins stirred widdershins
A Giant's big toe nail
Second hand spells used only once
New ones that can't fail.
Spells to grow some donkey's ears
On the teacher no one likes
Spells to make you good at sums
Spells to find lost bikes.

Spells that grow
And stretch and shrink
Spells that make
Your best friend stink
Stacks of spells
Stacked on my shelves
Come on in, see for yourselves
Magic prices, bargains galore
At Harry Hobgoblin's Superstore.

THE DOOR

RICHARD EDWARDS

A white door in the hawthorn hedge –
Who lives through there?
A sorcerer? A wicked witch
With serpents in her hair?

A king enchanted into stone?
A lost princess?
A servant girl who works all night
Spinning a cobweb dress?

A queen with slippers made of ice?
I'd love to see.
A white door in a hawthorn hedge –
I wish I had a key.

THE OLD MAGICIAN
JEAN KENWARD

Listen . . .
the old Magician, Rain is running
his long, grey fingers
over the dreaming house . . .

You can hear him tapping the roof.

His silken silver
touches the grasses.
Rabbit and bird and mouse
know him. They find his tread
in the secret places,
and the green frog feels a magic
wetting his skin.

Listen . . .the old Magician, Rain is coming . . .
and the locked earth
opens her doors
to let him in.

MRS MOON
ROGER McGOUGH

Mrs Moon
sitting up in the sky
little old lady
rock-a-bye
with a ball of fading light
and silvery needles
knitting the night

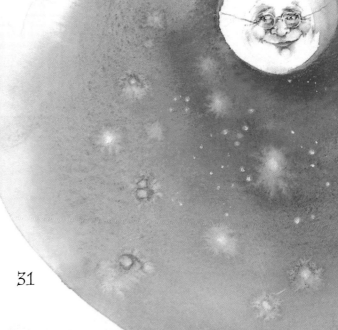

31

THE STAR COLLECTOR

GILLIAN FLOYD

One night, I went collecting stars
That sparkled big and bright.
I put them into old jam jars
And screwed the lids on tight.

I hid the jars in a safe place
A little while, and then
I took them from their secret space
To see my stars again.

I watched them as they shone and shone
And smiled to think that I
Had plucked them, one by one by one,
Out of the dark, dark sky.

But soon my stars began to fade:
They lost their lovely light –
So, knowing the mistake I'd made,
I ran into the night

And put them back into the sky –
The stars I thought were mine;
And now each night I stand below
And watch them shine and shine.

COBWEB MORNING

JUNE CREBBIN

On a Monday morning
We do spellings and Maths.
And silent reading.

But on the Monday
After the frost
We went straight outside.

Cobwebs hung in the cold air,
Everywhere.
All around the playground,
They clothed the trees,
Dressed every bush
In veils of fine white lace.

Each web,
A wheel of patient spinning.
Each spider,
Hidden,
Waiting.

Inside,
We worked all morning
To capture the outside.

Now
In our patterns and poems
We remember
The cobweb morning.

CALENDAR OF CLOUD
MOIRA ANDREW

A springtime cloud is
    sudden grief
    a sneak-thief
squeezing the morning dry.

A summer cloud is
    a wishbone
    a fishbone
filletted clean from sky.

An autumn cloud is
    a broomstick
    a doomstick
chasing cobwebs into night.

A winter cloud is
    a bucketful
    a ducking-stool
dowsing everything in sight.

MRS MAGEE
DENNIS LEE

    Mrs Magee
    Climbed into a tree,
And she only came down to go shopping.
    A branch was her bed,
    With a leaf on her head -
And whenever it rained, she got sopping.

THE NORTH WIND AND THE SOUTH WIND

GILLIAN FLOYD

THE NORTH WIND

I am the big, bad wind and I blow.
I come from the kingdom of coldness and snow,
Where polar bears shiver and icicles grow.

I am the big, bad wind and I **roar**.
I rattle your windows and batter your door
And scatter your papers all over the floor.

THE SOUTH WIND

I am the small, soft wind and I sigh.
I come from the land of sunshine and blue sky,
Where strange flowers bloom and exotic birds fly.

I am the small, soft wind and I *purr*.
I tickle your cheek and I ruffle your hair
And soothe you to sleep when there's nobody there.

IF I COULD ONLY TAKE HOME A SNOWFLAKE

JOHN AGARD

Snowflakes
like tiny
insects
drifting
down.

Without a hum
they come,
Without a hum
they go.

Snowflakes
like tiny
insects
drifting
down.

If only
I could take
one
home with me
to show
my friends
in the sun,
just for fun,
just for fun.

FLOWERING UMBRELLAS
STANLEY COOK

Umbrellas are folded up like buds.
But umbrella buds don't open in the sun.
They flower in the rain instead
In all kinds of colours: black, green and red,
Brown and white, and checked and striped.
Outside the school in the rain mothers stand
With umbrella flowers growing from their hands.

FROST
VALERIE BLOOM

Overnight, a giant spilt icing sugar on the ground,
He spilt it on the hedgerows, and the trees without a sound,
He made a wedding-cake of the haystack in the field,
He dredged the countryside and the grass was all concealed,
He sprinkled sugar on the roofs, in patches not too neat,
And in the morning when we woke, the world around was sweet.

SHE LIKES TO SWIM BENEATH THE SEA
Colin West

She likes to swim beneath the sea
And wear her rubber flippers,
She likes to dance outrageously
And wake up all the kippers.

PIRATE DON DURK OF DOWDEE
Mildred Meigs

Ho, for the Pirate Don Durk of Dowdee!
He was as wicked as wicked could be,
But oh, he was perfectly gorgeous to see!
    The Pirate Don Durk of Dowdee.

His conscience, of course, was black as a bat,
But he had a floppety plume on his hat,
And when he went walking it jiggled – like that!
    The plume of the Pirate Dowdee.

His coat it was crimson and cut with a slash,
And often as ever he twirled his moustache,
Deep down in the ocean the mermaids went splash,
    Because of Don Durk of Dowdee.

Moreover, Dowdee had a purple tattoo,
And stuck in his belt where he buckled it through
Were a dagger, a dirk and a squizzamaroo,
    For fierce was the Pirate Dowdee.

So fearful he was he would shoot at a puff,
And always at sea when the weather grew rough,
He drank from a bottle and wrote on his cuff,
    Did Pirate Don Durk of Dowdee.

Oh, he had a cutlass that swung at his thigh
And he had a parrot called Pepperkin Pye,
And a zigzaggy scar at the end of his eye
    Had Pirate Don Durk of Dowdee.

He kept in a cavern, this buccaneer bold,
A curious chest that was covered with mould,
And all of his pockets were jingly with gold!
    Oh, jing! Went the gold of Dowdee.

His conscience, of course, it was crook'd like a squash,
But both of his boots made a slickery slosh,
And he went through the world with a wonderful swash,
    Did Pirate Don Durk of Dowdee.

It's true he was wicked as wicked could be,
His sins they outnumbered a hundred and three,
But oh, he was perfectly gorgeous to see,
    The Pirate Don Durk of Dowdee.

THE DAY OF THE GULLS
JENNIFER CURRY

On a silver-cold day
Under snow-heavy clouds
The seagulls come
Driven inland
Swooping and screaming
Over the scraps in the gutters.

The children stare
As the street is made beautiful
By the white shining
Of their wings.

LIMPET
TED HUGHES

When big surf slams
His tower so hard
The Lighthouse-keeper's
Teeth are jarred.

The Limpet laughs
Beneath her hat:
'There's nothing I love
So much as that!

'Huge seas of shock
That roar to knock me
Off my rocker
Rock me, rock me.'

THE COTTAGE BY THE SEA

TONY MITTON

If you go there by day,
out to the ruined cottage
that sits on the cliff,
all you will find is silence.

Perhaps the wind
will pick at a broken shutter,
or maybe a gull
will cry as it flies overhead.

But if you go there by day,
all you will find is stillness
except for a scurry of ants,
or maybe a thrush
cracking a snail on a rock.

But if you go there by night
when the moon is low
and the mist drifts in from the sea,
you may find lights and music,
noises of joy and laughter
left over from lives gone by.

But then if you step through the door
to join with the fun,
everything vanishes, everything closes.
You'll find yourself standing alone,
amazed in the darkness,
with everything silent
and only the wind at your ear.

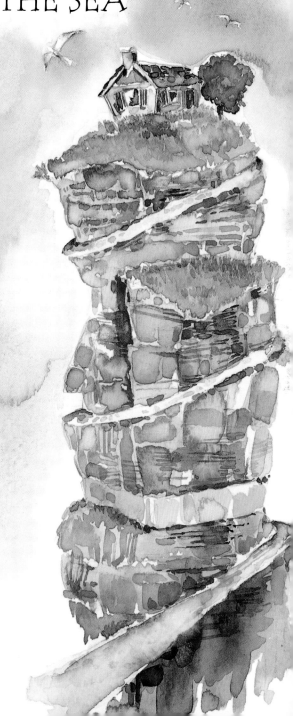

41

SECRETS
STEVE TURNER

I wrote a secret message
In lines of secret ink
So no one could discover
The secret words I think.

I took the secret message
When no one else was in
And secretly I hid it
Inside my secret tin.

I found a secret tree-trunk
Which held a secret fold
And slipped my secret package
Deep in the secret hole.

When I had grown much older
I sought the secret tree
To see if I could find the tin
Which held the secret me.

But all the trees looked taller
And changed a lot somehow.
They looked at me as if to say,
'Your secret's secret now.'

POEM FOR RODNEY
Nikki Giovanni

people always ask what
am i going to be
when i grow
up and i always
just think
i'd like to grow
up

THE NEW GIRL
Margot Tomes

I can feel
we're much the same,
though I don't
know your name.

What friends
we're going to be
when I know you
and you know me!

SCOWLING
Roger McGough

When I see you
scowling

I want to turn you
upside down

and see you smile!

TODAY IS VERY BORING

Jack Prelutsky

Today is very boring,
it's a very boring day,
there is nothing much to look at,
there is nothing much to say,
there's a peacock on my sneakers,
there's a penguin on my head,
there's a dormouse on my doorstep,
I am going back to bed.

Today is very boring,
it is boring through and through,
there is absolutely nothing,
that I think I want to do,
I see giants riding rhinos,
and an ogre with a sword,
there's a dragon blowing smoke rings,
I am positively bored.

Today is very boring,
I can hardly help but yawn,
there's a flying saucer landing
in the middle of my lawn,
a volcano just erupted
less than half a mile away,
and I think I felt an earthquake,
it's a very boring day.

WHAT DO YOU COLLECT?

Wes Magee

What do you collect?
Coins, dolls from other lands?
Or jokes
　　that no one understands?

What do you collect?
Stamps, gem-stones, model cars?
Or wrappers
　　ripped from chocolate bars?

What do you collect?
Skulls, posters, badges, bells?
Or walking sticks,
　　or seaside shells?

What do you collect?
Leaves, photographs of cats?
Or horror masks,
　　or party hats?

What do you collect?
Books, fossils, records, rocks?
Or comics
　　in a cardboard box?

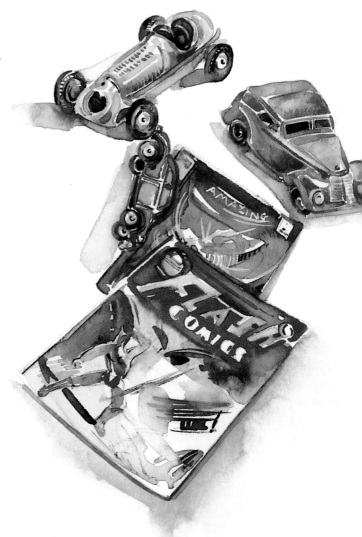

MR MARRUMPETER'S SHOP

RICHARD EDWARDS

In Mr Marrumpeter's junk shop
There is a peculiar clock,
It always strikes four
When you go in the door,
It sometimes says tick but it never says tock
In Mr Marrumpeter's shop.

In Mr Marrumpeter's junk shop
There's everything under the sun.
There's raffia and rope
And a box of black soap,
There's dubbin. There's even an elephant gun
In Mr Marrumpeter's shop.

In Mr Marrumpeter's junk shop
If I had a couple of weeks,
I'd find all the things
Worth a fortune, like rings
And ivory and silver and priceless antiques
In Mr Marrumpeter's shop.

In Mr Marrumpeter's junk shop
I've seen an Arabian knife,
A map of the moon
And a left handed spoon,
A tap from Peru
And some Mexican glue,
The reins for a goat
And an Eskimo's boat,
A shark's fin, some creels,
A case of stuffed eels,

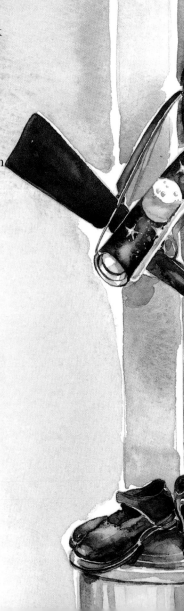

A buffalo bell
And some bagpipes as well,
Oh, I wish I could spend every day of my life
In Mr Marrumpeter's shop.

47

DREAMING
GERVASE PHINN

In the corner of the classroom,
A small child stared at the stuffed hedgehog
In the glass case.
'What are you thinking of?' asked the school inspector.
'I was just wondering,' the child replied wistfully,
'What it was doing… before it was stuffed!'

THE BOY WHOSE IMAGINATION RAN AWAY WITH HIM
LINDSAY MACRAE

For such a short boy,
Anthony Wriggly told some very tall tales:

Like the one about …
His gym shoes being stolen by Martians
His dog, Roger, winning the Grand National
His dad growing up in the only igloo in Rotherham
And his gran having flippers instead of feet.

The teacher warned him:
'Anthony, you must try not to let your imagination
run away with you!'

But one day it did.

It took him to a semi-detached kennel in the middle of nowhere
which was owned by a large, and unfriendly, talking biscuit.

And then it left him there.

WILL'S POEM

Biddy Woolston (with apologies to Irene McLeod)

I'm a hunky dog, a chunky dog, a fluffy black and tan
A soppy dog, a poppet dog, and a friend to every fan
But some say 'Oh a Rotty!' and quickly cross the street
Just shows they don't know me – I'm really very sweet!

Once I was a stray dog, lost in Worcester Park
Didn't know where I came from and frightened of the dark
Then it was the Dogs' Home, a cage with such cold floors
One day I was RESCUED – and landed on my paws!

Now I've a warm bed, and Horlicks as a nightcap
Biscuits and lovely meals – I am a lucky chap!
I've ball games and long walks, I chase squirrels up our tree
I've car rides and ice creams – and swimming in the sea!

HOTROD DOG

MAX FATCHEN

Now when we drive the family car
We rattle and roar and chug,
But our dog wants a window seat
And our dog wants the rug.

Our dog barks impatiently,
That's if we drive too slow.
Our dog whines at the traffic lights
Until the green says go.

Our dog watches the lorries pass
While vans are his delight.
He barks when we are veering left,
He yaps when we turn right.

His whining and his yelping make
My father lose his head.
No wonder that he didn't see
The traffic light turn red.

The cruising police patrol will glare.
My father's no road hog.
He simply says he cannot bear
Our back-seat driving dog.

VINCE THE CONFUSED ALSATIAN

LINDSAY MACRAE

Vince was meant to be a guard dog:
vicious, mean with lots of nous
But he was completely useless
if you broke into his house.

For Vince thought he was a rabbit
he loved lettuce and his hutch
And though he twitched his nose aggressively
he didn't bark that much.

THE 'VEGGY' LION

Spike Milligan

I'm a vegetarian Lion,
I've given up all meat,
I've given up all roaring
All I do is go tweet-tweet.

I never ever sink my claws
Into some animal's skin,
It only lets the blood run out
And lets the germs rush in.

I used to be ferocious,
I even tried to kill!
But the sight of all that blood
Made me feel quite ill.

I once attacked an Elephant
I sprang straight at his head.
I woke up three days later
In a Jungle hospital bed.

Now I just eat carrots,
They're easier to kill,
'Cos when I pounce upon them,
They all remain quite still!

MOTHER ALLIGATOR'S ADVICE TO HER CHILDREN

JOHN AGARD

Don't eat too much sweet
You'll spoil your lovely teeth.

Don't touch jelly or treacle
Stick to eating people.

THE THING ABOUT AARDVARKS

LINDSAY MACRAE

If you put them in a football team
they wouldn't score a goal
If you took them to a golf course
they'd never find the hole
If they're boxing with a squirrel
they'll come back badly beaten
They cannot win Monopoly
even if they're cheating
If someone let a stink-bomb off
they'd be the last to smell it
If you ask them to write down their name
they'll ask *you* how to spell it.

And even in the 'egg & spoon'
they're bringing up the rear
They never break the finishing tape
to hear a thunderous cheer
And yet there is place
where they are sure of victory
For the aardvark always comes first
in the English dictionary.

AR-A-RAT

Grace Nichols

I know a rat on Ararat,
He isn't thin, he isn't fat
Never been chased by any cat
Not that rat on Ararat.
He's sitting high on a mountain breeze,
Never tasted any cheese,
Never chewed up any old hat,
Not that rat on Ararat.
He just sits alone on a mountain breeze,
Wonders why the trees are green,
Ponders why the ground is flat,
O that rat on Ararat.
His eyes like saucers, glow in the dark –
The last to slip from Noah's ark.

MR GIRAFFE

Geoffrey Lapage

O Mister Giraffe, you make me laugh,
You seem to be made all wrong;
Your head is so high up there in the sky
And your neck is so very long
That your dinner and tea, it seems to me,
Have such a long way to go,
And I'm wondering how they manage to know
The way to your tummy below.

LOOKING AT
AN ELEPHANT
ANN BONNER

That elephant is
unbelievably
big
enormously
huge
wondrously
wide
tremendously
tall

while I
am decidedly
small.

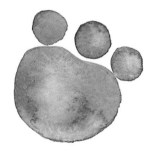

RACCOON
MARGOT TOMES

Raccoon,
with your black ringed eyes
and tiny paws,
startled at your work,
to you my garbage can
is full
of treasure.

AFTER BREAKFAST

ROY FULLER

I stop myself sliding a morsel
Of bacon fat into the bin.
It will do as a meal for the robin,
His legs are so terribly thin.

THE FUNNY BEASTS

ANONYMOUS

Have you seen the elephant
  Counting out his money?
Have you seen a limpet
  Eating bread and honey?
Or a striped hyena
  Hanging out the clothes,
With a native oyster
  Snapping off his nose?

Have you seen the crocodile,
  With a pocket full of rye?
Or a nest of water-rats
  Baked in a pie?
Or some sixty lizards
  Who'd just begun to sing?
Or a tabby cat, as a dainty dish
  Set before the king?

A FARMYARD SONG

TRADITIONAL

I had a cat and the cat pleased me,
I fed my cat by yonder tree;
    Cat goes fiddle-i-fee.

I had a hen and the hen pleased me,
I fed my hen by yonder tree;
    Hen goes chimmy-chuck, chimmy-chuck,
    Cat goes fiddle-i-fee.

I had a duck and the duck pleased me,
I fed my duck by yonder tree;
    Duck goes quack, quack,
    Hen goes chimmy-chuck, chimmy-chuck,
    Cat goes fiddle-i-fee.

I had a goose and the goose pleased me,
I fed my goose by yonder tree;
    Goose goes swishy, swashy,
    Duck goes quack, quack,
    Hen goes chimmy-chuck, chimmy-chuck,
    Cat goes fiddle-i-fee.

I had a sheep and the sheep pleased me,
I fed my sheep by yonder tree;
    Sheep goes baa, baa,
    Goose goes swishy, swashy,
    Duck goes quack, quack,
    Hen goes chimmy-chuck, chimmy-chuck,
    Cat goes fiddle-i-fee.

I had a pig and the pig pleased me,
I fed my pig by yonder tree;
    Pig goes griffy, gruffy,
    Sheep goes baa, baa,

Goose goes swishy, swashy,
Duck goes quack, quack,
Hen goes chimmy-chuck, chimmy-chuck,
Cat goes fiddle-i-fee.

I had a cow and the cow pleased me,
I fed my cow by yonder tree;
　　Cow goes moo, moo,
　　Pig goes griffy, gruffy,
　　Sheep goes baa, baa,
　　Goose goes swishy, swashy,
　　Duck goes quack, quack,
　　Hen goes chimmy-chuck, chimmy-chuck,
　　Cat goes fiddle-i-fee.

I had a horse and the horse pleased me,
I fed my horse by yonder tree;
　　Horse goes neigh, neigh,
　　Cow goes moo, moo,
　　Pig goes griffy, gruffy,
　　Sheep goes baa, baa,
　　Goose goes swishy, swashy,
　　Duck goes quack, quack,
　　Hen goes chimmy-chuck, chimmy-chuck,
　　Cat goes fiddle-i-fee.

I had a dog and the dog pleased me,
I fed my dog by yonder tree;
　　Dog goes bow-wow, bow-wow,
　　Horse goes neigh, neigh,
　　Cow goes moo, moo,
　　Pig goes griffy, gruffy,
　　Sheep goes baa, baa,
　　Goose goes swishy, swashy,
　　Duck goes quack, quack,
　　Hen goes chimmy-chuck, chimmy-chuck,
　　Cat goes fiddle-i-fee.

58

GINGER

Irene Rawnsley

Mrs Garter who lives
at twenty-nine
has a ginger cat
who is very fine.

In fact, he is absolutely enormous!

I heard Mrs Garter
tell my mum
that he weighs two stones;
I can believe it.

That cat must be a record-breaker!

Each evening
when we're playing out,
Mrs Garter shouts
to him, 'Ginger!'

He knows his name, but he doesn't go running.

Standing there
with her little dish,
she calls, 'Ginger,
come for your lovely fish!'

He sits round the corner, pretending not to hear.

He can afford to wait
because he's already
had one tea
with us,
and one at Ashworth's
and at Kenworthy's,
and Binns',
and a few scraps at Bakers' ...

CAT ALERT!
SANDY BROWNJOHN

Now listen, you cat with the question-mark tail
And claws that scrabble under the bed,
I know you enjoy chasing balls of foil
And that game of jumping right on my head;
I know it's fun to hide round the door
Then pounce on my slippers without any warning,
And I'm very fond of my face being licked –
But not at half past four in the morning!

NEXT DOOR'S CAT

Valerie Bloom

Next door's cat is by the pond
Sitting, waiting for the fish,
Next door's cat thinks Geraldine
Would make a tasty dish.

He's had Twinkle and Rose Red,
He ate Alberta too,
And all we found were Junior's bones
When that horrid cat was through.

Next door's cat comes round at night,
Strikes when we're in bed,
In the morning when we wake
Another fish is dead.

Next door's cat has seen the new fish,
He thinks that it's a goner,
What a surprise he's going to get,
When he finds it's a piranha.

A CONVERSATION WITH A CAT

GILLIAN FLOYD

Greymalkin, Greymalkin, say, where have you been?

I've been to the forest all gloomy and green,
I've been to the forest all dusky and dense,
The magical forest, so dark and immense.

Greymalkin, Greymalkin, say, what did you see?

I saw an owl blink in the branch of a tree,
I saw the moon ride through the fields of the sky,
Just like a white horse that goes cantering by.

Greymalkin, Greymalkin, what did you do?

I danced to the song of the wind as it blew,
I danced to the song of the wind through the trees,
The song of the beautiful, musical breeze.

Greymalkin, Greymalkin, say, my little pet,
Come, sit on my lap and I'll make you forget
The magical forest, the owl in the trees,
The cantering moon and the musical breeze.

I'll sit on your lap, but I will not forget
The forest where I will go dancing in yet,
The forest where I will tonight again be,
The magical forest that's waiting for me.

NIGHT CREATURES

Pauline Stewart

Lizards licking
crickets cricking
bats flapping
snakes slipping
owls scowl
dogs howl
chickens flurry
mongoose hurry
spiders sneaking
frogs creaking
mosquitoes sipping
rats ripping.
'GOODNIGHT!'

ZINGA, ZINGA

Dennis Lee

Zinga, zinga, zumpkin:
A pussy on a pumpkin.
   A puss in the light
    But a witch at night!
Zinga, zinga, zumpkin.

AT NIGHT
AILEEN FISHER

When night is dark
my cat is wise
to light the lanterns
in his eyes.

SCARED OF THE DARK
VALERIE BLOOM

I'm scared of the dark
I don't like it one bit,
I'm scared of the dark,
There, I've admitted it.

I'm scared of the things
That go bump in the night,
I'm scared of the creatures
Outside of the light.

I'm scared of the dark,
And what scares me the most,
Is when in the dark
I meet another ghost.

GHOSTS?

IRENE RAWNSLEY

Of course there's ghosts; old houses
are full of them; folk don't disappear
completely after they move away;
traces of them remain

trapped inside forever, waiting
night time chances to come alive.
It only needs the wind to wake,
soot to settle, a few dust curls

to slip across an empty floor;
there'll be the scratch of pens
on football coupons; knitting needles,
dominoes clicking, everything

they liked to do before they moved away.
Listen for ghosts tonight; you'll catch
faint happenings in darkness;
hold your breath, you'll hear them.

WHEN I CLOSE MY EYES

Andrew Collett

When I close my eyes at night,
Lying in my bed,
My pillow fills with stories.
Legends fill my bed.

Stories of mighty kings
And giants running tall,
Legends of fierce monsters
And fairies very small.

Stories from China,
Where dragons never die,
And legends from India
Where elephants can fly.

When I close my eyes at night,
Lying in my bed,
My pillow fills with stories.
Legends fill my bed.

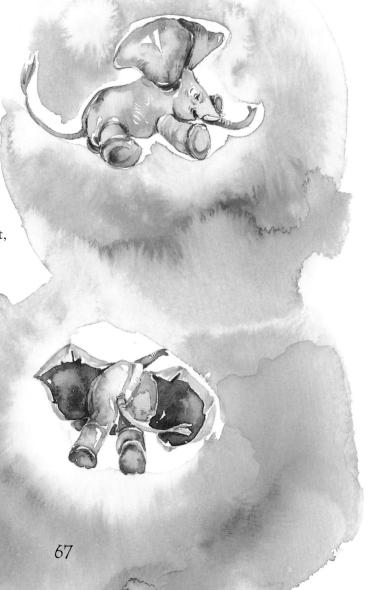

CANDLE
BRIAN MORSE

The night of the power cut,
when everything went off,
they put a candle in my room.
I went to sleep by candle light.

Every time I woke
the candle's soft light
was flickering
on the chest of drawers.

It lit my dreams.

SLEEPING OUTDOORS
MARCHETTE CHUTE

Under the dark
is a star,
Under the star
is a tree,
Under the tree
is a blanket,
And under the blanket
is me.

TIME TO GET UP

FRED SEDGWICK

Light is creeping round the curtain
    To the corner of my bed.
It creeps along the bedroom wall
    And creeps up to my head.

People talk and engines hum.
    There's a busy street outside.
Out of bed! Walk to the window!
    Push it open wide!

Soon there's school and dressing up,
    Sand and water play.
Soon there's all my friends again
    And another day.

HAIR GROWING

SUE COWLING

Hair grows a centimetre a month
Or a third of a millimetre a day.
That means
That while you've been reading this poem
Your hair
(And mine)
Will have grown
A billimetre,
A trillimetre,
A zillimetre
Or a squillimetre!
It depends how fast you read.

69

GETTING UP

John Row

Getting up is
    people shouting about the time!

Getting up is
    trying not to hear them!

Getting up is
    having your bedclothes pulled away!

Getting up is
    seeing if the legs still work
    as they hit the floor!

Getting up is
    seeing how little can be washed
    in how short a time!

Getting up is
    being asked five times
    if you have really done your hair!
    And being told your neck is still dirty
    but it's too late to do anything about it now!

Getting up is
    getting down to the one meal of the day
    you're allowed to rush.
    Breakfast!!

Getting up is
　　getting out when you still haven't found
　　the things you needed for the day!
Getting up is

　　　almost as bad

　　　　　as going

　　　　　　to bed!!

SHOELACES
SUE COWLING

Two laces,
Shoelaces –
Which way
To tie?
This way?
Or that way?
I wonder.

One loop,
Then two loops
Like rabbits' ears –
Try
Knotting them
Over
And under!

HEY DIDDLE DIDDLE

Andrew Fusek Peters

Wash your ears! Mum said,
So I took them off,
And stuck them in the washing machine.

Clean your room! Dad said,
So I rolled it up,
And shook it out of the window.

Make the breakfast! My brother said,
So I did –
With bits of balsa wood and modelling glue.

Feed the cat! My Auntie said,
So I fed him…
To the dog!

Take your time! Dad said.
So I packed up the clocks
And flew off to Mars
Where the days fly by,
Wearing nothing but stars!

OLD MRS LAZIBONES

Gerda Mayer

Old Mrs Lazibones
And her dirty daughter
Never used soap
And never used water.

        Higgledy piggledy cowpat
        What d'you think of that?

Daisies from their fingernails,
Birds' nests in their hair-O,
Dandelions from their ears -
What a dirty pair-O!

        Higgledy piggledy cowpat
        What d'you think of that?

Came a prince who sought a bride,
Riding past their doorstep,
Quick, said Mrs Lazibones,
Girl, under the watertap.

        Higgledy piggledy cowpat
        What d'you think of that?

Washed her up and washed her down,
Then she washed her sideways,
But the prince was far, far away,
He'd ridden off on the highways.

        Higgledy piggledy cowpat
        What d'you think of that?

SOAP
STANLEY COOK

Soap lives in water
And is hard to catch
Slipping through your fingers
Especially in the bath.

It hasn't a handle to hold
And can't be fastened with string;
It hasn't a zip to close
Or a cardboard box to go in.

It doesn't answer a whistle
Or come for milk or a biscuit;
It won't go into a kennel
Or curl up and sleep in a basket.

Soap is a square slippery fish:
I wish it would stay in its place
And not always vanish
While I'm washing my face.

BATH
PAULINE STEWART

Wash wash in the bath
even though I'm not dirty.
If I keep on washing every day
I'll be clean by the time I'm thirty.

HOT PANTS
Michael Rosen

The tumble-dryer
dries socks hot
and hot socks
make my toes warm.

All through winter

when it's wet and cold
our tumble-dryer
rumbles round.

Hot socks
hot shirts
hot skirts
hot pants

All through winter
in the wet and cold
I watch where the pipe from the dryer ends:

It's where there's a grille,
and through the holes
the dryer breathes out
hot air.

Hot air
hot breaths
hot puffs
hot pants.

WHEN I'M OLDER

Lemn Sissay

I'll never pull my socks up. I'll never fold my clothes
I'll even have a servant to wipe my drippy nose
And at the dinner table FIRST I'll have my sweet
I'll always rush my tea and never brush my teeth

I'll never wipe my face and never clean my shoes
I'll never cry never ever. I'll never flush the loo
I'll never do my homework. I'll never eat sprouts
When Mum asks 'where you going' I'll say 'OUT'

I'll never clean my bedroom, never change my socks
I'll always yell 'OI!' through the letterbox
I'll never wash the pots. I'll never do my bed.
For breakfast I'll only eat jam on shortbread

I'll never wipe my feet, I'll never wipe my nose
I'll never cut my nails and I'll never wash my clothes
I'll always ring the doorbell, I'll never wear a tie
I'll always answer the telephone with the word

                                        Goodbye!

THE CAT'S PYJAMAS

Irene Rawnsley

*This bedroom looks like
there's been an earthquake!
Tidy everything away, right now.*

I can't, Mum.
It's Wizard Wondro's Infernal Castle Trap
for melting mean monsters.
You're standing in it.

*And put the tops on those felt tip pens.
They'll go dry.*

There're ray guns to scorch beams of light
across the path of enemies
who approach the drawbridge.

*Isn't that your homework book?
Pick it up from the rug.*

It's a secret coded message from Wizard Wondro
to guide his followers
across the evil swamp.

*I suppose those are Wizard Wondro's pyjamas.
Put them in the drawer.*

They're not Wizard Wondro's.
He wears invisible magic armour,
proof against all weapons
yet light enough to fly in.

Then whose pyjamas are they?

Er…I expect they belong to the cat.

OUR COCONUT MAT

Colin West

We have a mat
Of coconut
At our front door
With WELCOME on it.

And everyone
Who enters our house
Is welcomed in
By our coconut mat.

But when somebody comes
I'd rather not see,
I turn around
Our coconut mat.

So when they leave,
To face the rain,
They're welcomed out
By our coconut mat.

TRAFFIC CONES (OR ARE THEY?)
SUE COWLING

There are many more now
Than there were yesterday –
Pointy
Stripy aliens
Blocking off the way,
Telling us we can't go
Where we wanted to –
Aliens
Coming soon
To a road near you!

RED
STANLEY COOK

Red is loud and shouts,
The colour of fire engines
And the topmost traffic light.
Red asks people to notice
Cones round holes in the road;
Red cherries and strawberries
And hips and haws
Ask for notice
From the birds.
When I'm painting,
Red is the colour I like best
And use more often than the rest.

79

EARTH EATER
Brian Morse

The digger
puts its
yellow chin
on the ground
and pushes.

With
a clank
its neck
jerks up.
For a moment
it thinks
then
slowly,
as if it was tasting,
eats
a mouthful
of earth.

Ugh! That
tasted horrid!
Its long neck
swings,
looking for
a place
to put it
down
as fast as it can.
It finds it
and tips
the earth
in a pile.
That's better!
But the man
in the cab
says,
'Hey! No rest for you!
There's more where that came from!'

At night
the driver
parks it
with its chin
on the ground,
looking at all
that earth.

I think
it's a sad life
for a digger.

YELLOW DOOR

Michael Rosen

I've often wondered
where gas comes from.

Now I know.

I was walking down the street
and I looked down
at the pavement
and I saw
a little yellow door.

I thought:
why is there
a little yellow door
in the middle of the pavement?

And then I saw it.

On the door
it said:
'GAS'.

Now I know where
gas comes from.

TELEVISION AERIALS

STANLEY COOK

Television aerials
Look like witches' brooms.
When they finish flying
They leave them on the roof.

Television aerials
Are sticks to prod the sky
To make clouds full of rain
Hurry by.

Television aerials
Reach above the chimney tops
To make a perch
Where tired birds can stop.

Television aerials
Are fixed to the chimney side
To rake us songs and pictures
Out of the sky.

SOUNDS
STEWART HENDERSON

Crunching ginger biscuits
is like hearing soldiers tread,
marching over gravel
on the inside of your head.

Chewing a marshmallow
is nowhere near as loud.
It's the smaller, sweet equivalent
of swallowing a cloud.

JEREMY BISHOP
VALERIE BLOOM

Jeremy, Jeremy Bishop,
Was a good boy, he ate all his fishop,
When he was done,
Like a well-brought up son,
He washed and dried his dishop.

ETHEL READ A BOOK
COLIN WEST

Ethel read, Ethel read,
Ethel read a book.
Ethel read a book in bed,
She read a book on Ethelred.
The book that Ethel read in bed,
(The book on Ethelred) was red.
The book was red that Ethel read,
In bed on Ethelred.

malinger

BIG WORDS
DAVID SCOTT

Popocatepetl

I like big words
it doesn't matter what they mean.
The bigger they are the better,
the biggest you've ever seen.

I search them out
in dictionaries and atlases
and backs of cereal packets
and then a lot of practice

Kanchenjunga

to get my tongue round
Popocatepetl
or my nose round Kanchenjunga
or my mouth round malinger
or my teeth round spittle.

spittle

THOR THE GOD OF THUNDER
ANONYMOUS

Thor the God of Thunder
was riding on his filly,
'I'm Thor!' he cried.
The horse replied,
'Well get a thaddle thilly!'

85

'AND THEN'

June Crebbin

My teacher says
I mustn't say
'And then',
Like when I write,
'I went into the forest
And then I saw a huge bear
And then the huge bear
Lumbered towards me
And then I grabbed him
By the throat
And then...'
My teacher says
Every now
And then
I should stop.

But I don't know when.

And if I did
I might not get started again

And then
I'd never finish the story.

DON'T

RICHARD EDWARDS

Why do people say 'don't' so much,
Whenever you try something new?
It's more fun doing than don'ting,
So why don't people say "do"?

Don't slurp your spaghetti
Don't kiss that cat
Don't butter your fingers
Don't walk like that
Don't wash your books
Don't bubble your tea
Don't jump on your sister
Don't goggle at me
Don't climb up the curtains
Don't feed the chair
Don't sleep in your wardrobe
Don't cut off your hair
Don't draw on the pillow
Don't change all the clocks
Don't water the 'phone
Don't hide my socks
Don't cycle upstairs
Don't write on the eggs
Don't chew your pyjamas
Don't paint your legs…

Oh, why do people say 'don't' so much,
Whenever you try something new?
It's more fun doing than don'ting,
So why don't people say 'do'?

BRENDA BAKER
DOUG MACLEOD

Brenda Baker, quite ill-bred,
Used to cuddle fish in bed.
Tuna, trout and conger-eels,
Salmon, sole and sometimes seals.
Barracuda, bream and bass,
She cuddled them until - alas!
One unforgotten Friday night
She slept with two piranhas,
And, being rather impolite,
They ate her best pyjamas!

ROBIN THE BOBBIN
TRADITIONAL

Robin the Bobbin, the big-bellied Ben,
He ate more meat than fourscore men;
He ate a cow, he ate a calf,
He ate a butcher and a half;
He ate a church, he ate a steeple,
He ate the priest and all the people!
    A cow and a calf,
    An ox and a half,
    A church and a steeple,
    And all the good people,
And yet he complain'd that his stomach wasn't full.

TWELVE HUNTSMEN

ANONYMOUS

Twelve huntsmen with horns and hounds,
Hunting over other men's grounds!
Eleven ships sailing o'er the main,
Some bound for France and some for Spain;
I wish them all safe home again.
Ten comets in the sky,
Some low and some high;
Nine peacocks in the air,
I wonder how they all came there,
I do not know and I do not care.
Eight joiners in a joiners' hall,
Working with the tools and all;
Seven lobsters in a dish,
As fresh as any heart could wish;
Six beetles against the wall,
Close by an old woman's apple stall;
Five puppies of our dog Ball,
Who daily for their breakfast call;
Four horses stuck in a bog,
Three monkeys tied to a clog;
Two pudding ends would choke a dog,
With a gaping wide-mouthed waddling frog.

THE QUEEN OF EVERYWHERE

GILLIAN FLOYD

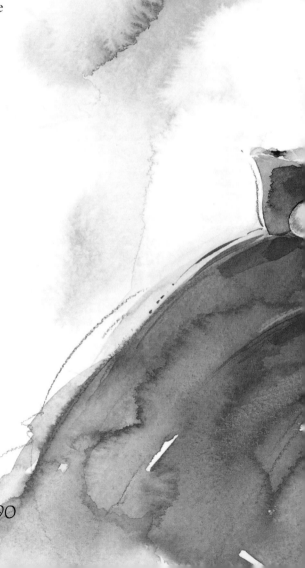

I AM THE Queen of Everywhere,
I wear red ribbons in my hair
And yellow stockings on my legs.
My dress is made of Easter Eggs,

My crown is made from Birthday Cake
And when I'm hungry I can break
A piece right off and eat it up.
I drink milk from a china cup

And tea out of a leather shoe.
I like to say How do you do?
To everybody that I meet
When I'm out walking in the street.

If I should ever pass your way
Don't be afraid: just smile and say
Your beauty is beyond compare,
Your Highness, Queen of Everywhere!

Author Index

Acknowledgements

For permission to use copyright material, the editor and publisher gratefully acknowledge the following:

John Agard: 'If Only I Could Take Home a Snowflake' and 'Mother Alligator's Advice to Her Children' from I Din Do Nuttin by John Agard, published by Bodley Head. Used by permission of the Random House Group Limited. **Ann Bonner:** 'Looking at an Elephant', copyright Ann Bonner. First published in Green Poems, OUP, Jill Bennett. **Sandy Brownjohn:** 'Cat Alert!' © Sandy Brownjohn from In and Out of the Shadows (OUP). **Barry Buckingham:** 'Oh Dear, Mum!' by permission of Barry Buckingham. **Charles Causley:** 'Green Man in the Garden' by Charles Causley from Collected Poems, as published by Macmillan. By permission of David Higham Associates. **Andrew Collett:** 'When I Close My Eyes'. By permission of Andrew Collett, **Sue Cowling:** 'Hair Growing', first published in Poetry Parade – Kersplosh, Kersplash, Kersplat!, Oxford University Press, 2001. 'Traffic Cones (Or Are They?)' and 'Shoelaces'. By permission of the author, Sue Cowling. **June Crebbin:** 'And then'. By permission of the author, June Crebbin, from The Jungle Sale (Viking 1988). **Jennifer Curry:** 'The Day of the Gulls' copyright Jennifer Curry, from Down Our Street, by Jennifer and Graeme Curry, published by Methuen Childrens Books in 1988.

Berlie Doherty: 'Grandpa' from Walking On Air, published by HarperCollins. By permission of David Higham Associates. **Richard Edwards:** 'The Door', 'Mr Marrumpter's Shop' and 'Don't' from The Word Party. By permission of The Lutterworth Press. **Max Fatchen:** 'Hotrod Dog' copyright © Max Fatchen. Reproduced by permission of John Johnson Ltd. **Gillian Floyd:** 'A Conversation With a Cat', 'The Queen of Everywhere', 'The North Wind and the South Wind' and 'The Star Collector'. By permission of Gillian Floyd. **John Foster:** 'Grandad's Clothes' © 1997 John Foster from Making Waves (Oxford University Press). Included by permission of the author. **Nikki Giovanni:** 'Poem for Rodney' from Spin a Soft Black Song by Nikki Giovanni. By permission of Farrar, Strauss & Giroux, LLC. **David Harmer:** 'Harry Hobgoblin's Superstore' from Creaking Down the Corridor, A Twist in the Tale, 1993. © David Harman. By permission of David Harman. **Stewart Henderson:** 'Sounds' by Stewart Henderson © 2000. From the collection Who Left Grandad at the Chipshop? published by Lion Books. **Ted Hughes:** 'Limpet' from The Mermaid's Purse, published by Faber and Faber Ltd. By permission of Faber and Faber Ltd. **Jean Kenward:** ''The Great White Horse' from Horse Poems, OUP, 1990. **James Kirkup:** 'Unicorn'. With thanks to James Kirkup and Salzburg University Press. **Lindsay MacRae:** 'The Babysitter' and 'The

Wicked Stepmother' from How to Avoid Kissing Your Parents in Public, Penguin 2001. By permission of A.P. Watt Limited on behalf of Lindsay MacRae. 'The Boy Whose Imagination Ran Away With Him', 'Vince the Confused Alsatian' and 'The Thing about Aardvarks', first published in You Cannay Shove Yer Granny off a Bus!, Viking 1995. Reproduced by permission of The Agency (London) Ltd. Text copyright © Lindsay MacRae 1995. **Roger McGough:** 'Mrs Moon' © Roger McGough from Sky in the Pie as published by Kestrel. 'Pillow Talk' from Scowling as published by Viking. Reprinted by permission of PFD on behalf of: Roger McGough. **Colin McNaughton:** 'I Planted Some Seeds' from There's an Awful Lot of Weirdos in Our Neighbourhood. Text & illustrations © 1987 Colin McNaughton. Reproduced by permission of the publisher, Walker Books Ltd., London. **Wes Magee:** 'What Do You Collect?' from The Witch's Brew and Other Poems, published by Cambridge University Press in 1989. By permission of Cambridge University Press. **Gerda Mayer:** 'Old Mrs Lazibones' © Gerda Mayer. First published in The Knockabout Show, Chatto & Windus, 1978. Now in Bonnini's Cat, Iron Press, 1999. **Tony Mitton:** 'The Cottage by the Sea', 'Magic Carpet', 'What is Under?' and 'Instructions for Growing Poetry' from Plum, as published by Scholastic Children's Books. By permission of David Higham Associates. **Brian Morse:** 'Earth Eater' © text Brian Morse 1994, taken from Plenty of Time Bodley Head. By permission of the author c/o Rogers, Coleridge and White, London. **Grace Nichols:** 'Ar-a-Rat'. Reproduced with permission of Curtis Brown Ltd London on behalf of Grace Nichols. Copyright © Grace Nichols, 1991. **Brian Patten:** 'Earwings' © Brian Patten, 2000. From Juggling with Gerbils, first published in 2000 by Puffin Books. Reprinted by permission of the author c/o Rogers, Coleridge and White, 20 Powis Mews, London W11 1TN. **Andrew and Polly Fusek Peters:** 'Mum' and 'Dad' from Sadderday and Funday, Reproduced by permission of Hodder and Stoughton Limited. 'Hey Diddle Diddle' from The Moon in on the Microphone, Sherbourne Publications, 1997. By permission of Andrew Fusek Peters. **Gervase Phinn:** 'My Monstrous Bear' from It Takes One to Know One, Penguin, 2001. 'Dreaming', from Classroom Creatures, Roselea Publications, 1996. By permission of Gervase Phinn. **Joan Poulson:** 'Dragonflies'. First published in A Glass of Fresh Air (Collins Educational 1996), copyright © Joan Poulson 1996. Reprinted by permission of the author. **Jack Prelutsky:** 'Today is Very Boring' from The New Kid on the Block © Jack Prelutsky, 1984. Published by Egmont Books, London and used with permission. **Irene Rawnsley:** 'The Cat's Pyjamas', from the House of a Hundred Cats, Methuen Children's Books, 1995. 'Ghosts', from Hiding Out Smith, Doorstep Books, Huddersfield, 1996. 'Ginger', from Ask a Silly Question, Methuen Children's Books, 1988. By permission of Irene Rawnsley.

Michael Rosen: 'Hot Pants'. Reprinted by permission of PFD on behalf of Michael Rosen. © Michael Rosen. **John Row:** 'Getting up' by John Row from The Pong Machine, Annis Press 1999. **David Scott:** 'Big Words' from How Does It Feel? by David Scott (Blackie, 1989). Copyright © David Scott, 1989. **Fred Sedgwick:** 'Time to Get Up'. By permission of Fred Sedgwick. **Lemn Sissay:** 'When I'm Older' from The Emperor's Watchmaker, published by Bloomsbury. By permission of David Higham Associates Limited. **Rowena Somerville:** 'The Martians Have Taken My Brother' from The Martians Have Taken My Brother by Rowena Sommerville, published by Hutchinson. Used by permission of the Random House Group Limited. **Pauline Stewart:** 'Night Creatures' and 'Bath' from Singing Down the Breadfruit by Pauline Stewart, published by Bodley Head. Used by permission of the Random House Group Limited. **Colin West:** 'Ethel Read a Book', 'She Likes to Swim Beneath the Sea' and 'Our Coconut Mat' © Colin West. Reprinted with permission of the author. **Jeanne Willis:** 'Potting Shed' from Toffee Pockets by Jeanne Willis, published by Bodley Head. Used by permission of The Random House Group Limited. **Biddy Woolston:** 'Will's Poem'. By permission of Biddy Woolston.

Every effort has been made to trace the copyright holders but in some cases this has not proved possible. The publisher will be happy to rectify any such errors or omissions in future reprints and/or new editions.